Led By The Spirit

Wiley E. Hughes

[2]

DEDICATION

This is my fifth book. John Maxwell said he was once asked how he got to have a book he authored on the New York Time's Best Seller's list. He replied, "I have written over 50 books. Can you name me one of my first 30?" I have dedicated my previous books to some very special people in my life. Because of the topic of this book, I would like to dedicate it to my wonderful parents, Howard and Ann Hughes. I love you so much mom and dad!

[4]

Contents

Introduction/Page 7

Spirit-led living in the 21st Century/Page 13

Spirit-led thinking in the 21st Century/Page 37

Spiritual Leadership "Shepherds"/Page 53

Powerful Leadership "The Holy Spirit"/Page 107

The "Sweet Life"/Page 147

Bibliography/Page 157

[6]

Introduction

No one can effectively lead if someone isn't willing to follow. I believe that neither the ills of society nor the problems individuals face daily are a result of the lack of leadership in the world. To me it seems that the problems many people face today have more to do with their unwillingness to be led, instructed, and mentored than they do with a lack of good leadership. I do believe, however, that the struggles and stresses many people face everyday would become more infrequent if they would learn the value of humility and service.

Favor and blessing are the byproducts of honest, humble, and loyal service to others.

Years ago a humble minister served a church in a small country town. His ministry was quiet, and few souls were brought to Christ there. Year after year, the work became more and more discouraging. It was only years later that the faithful pastor found great joy in the knowledge that one of those he had won to Christ was Charles Haddon Spurgeon, the great preacher, who was later used by God to bring multitudes to his Son. Humble service is rewarded now and certainly will be rewarded even more when Christ comes.[1]

A willingness to be led by others helps us learn how to be led by the Holy Spirit. The Spirit of God makes no one follow His leadership. Every man and woman has the God-given right to choose who they will humble themselves to and serve. Joshua makes it clear who he and his family chose to serve in Joshua 24. In verse 15 of Joshua 24, Joshua says, *"But if serving the LORD seems undesirable to you, then choose for yourselves this day whom*

---

[1]"Rewards of Service," in *1500 Illustrations for Biblical Preaching* ed., Michael P. Green (Grand Rapids, MI: Baker 2001) 332.

you will serve, whether the gods your forefathers served beyond the River, or the gods of the Amorites, in whose land you are living. But as for me and my household, we will serve the LORD." [2]

This invitation of Joshua is similar to that extended by Moses to Israel on the other side of the Jordan. (Deut. 30: 15-20). He recognized that one can only serve God in sincerity and truth if he has freely and willingly pledged in his

---

[2] Unless otherwise indicated all Bible references in this book are to the New International Version– Updated (NIV) (Grand Rapids: Zondervan, 1984).

heart to do so. In verse 15 of Joshua 24, he summarizes the options that are open to Israel: (1) they could return to serve the gods of their ancestors, (2) they could serve the gods of the Amorites, or (3) they could follow the example of him and his family, i.e., to serve the Lord. According to Spiros Zodhiates, this stands as one of the great affirmations of faith in all the Bible.[3]

I have discovered, in my 20+ years of vocational ministry, that there are still many Christian people who have not made such an

---

[3] "Study Notes," *Key Word Study Bible*, ed., Spiros Zodhiates (Chattanooga, TN: AMG 1990) 324-235.

affirmation, the decision to be Spirit led. In contrast, they too often allow their desires, feelings, preferences, and personal ambitions to prompt their actions. You may be asking how one can be a Christian and not be Spirit led. If so, then you are asking the key question at the center of the premise of this book. "Can we be Christian and be led by our flesh most of the time? I believe we can and I believe the Bible addresses the struggle between what we want to do and what we know we should do. The good news is, we CAN be Spirit led and the result is awesome.

CHAPTER 1

Spirit-Led Living in the 21st Century

One of the most poignant and scholarly books recently written, in my opinion, on the subject of being Spirit Led is Thompson K. Mathew's book, "Spirit-Led Ministry in the 21st Century." Mathew states that "Scripture defines ministry as being a co-worker with God, carrying out His purposes in the world."[4] With the abundant life given to us when we are born-again, it is tempting for us to lose sight of the purpose of that new life.

God's plan for the redeemed is to love others through us. A story I heard recently

---

[4]Thompson K. Mathew, "Ministry Defined," in *Spirit-Led Ministry in the 21st Century* (Xulon Press 2004) 18.

illustrates this quite well. Jimmy was a new Christian who regularly helped the homeless in the community around the church he attended. On one particular night, the church was holding a mid-week bible study. Near the end of the service, one of the local homeless people walked up to the altar for prayer. The minister asked him if he would like to get to know Jesus. The man replied, "Is he like Jimmy?" The best way to live Spirit-led lives is to take a closer look at how Jesus lived his life. His Spirit-led living in the first century can be a prime example for Spirit led living in the 21st century.

Matthew 4 begins with Jesus being led by the Spirit into the desert to be tempted by the devil. In verse 2-11, Matthew writes, *"After fasting forty days and forty nights, he was hungry. 3 The tempter came to him and said, "If you are the Son of God, tell these stones to become bread." 4 Jesus answered, "It is written: 'Man does not live on bread alone, but on every word that comes from the mouth of God.'" 5 Then the devil took him to the holy city and had him stand on the highest point of the temple. 6 "If you are the Son of God," he said, "throw yourself down. For it is written: "'He will command his angels concerning you, and they will lift you up in their hands, so that you will not strike your foot against a stone.'" 7 Jesus answered him, "It is also written: 'Do not put the Lord your God to the test.'" 8 Again, the devil took him to a very high mountain and showed him all the kingdoms of the world and their splendor. 9 "All this I will give you," he said, "if you will bow down and worship me." 10 Jesus said to him, "Away from me, Satan! For it is written: 'Worship the Lord your God, and serve him only.'" 11 Then the devil left him, and angels came and attended him."* Spirit-led living will sometimes take us through times of temptation.

At the time of Christ's temptation in the desert, He was on His way to fulfilling His destiny. His destiny was to preach. According to Matthew 4:17, *"From that time on Jesus began to preach, 'Repent, for the kingdom of heaven is near'."* It is interesting how Jesus was led by the Spirit through a time of temptation just prior to Him preaching, which was what He came to earth to do. Spirit-led living in the 21st century will take us through temptation sometimes. It is crucial that we learn to persevere through those times in the desert. Often, it is to our self instead of the Spirit which we often listen during temptation. This causes a temporary paralysis of our spiritual senses. I call it suffering from spiritual "A.D.D" **Allowing Destiny Distractions**.

Notice in verse 3 how Satan endeavored to distract Jesus from His mission by appealing to His hunger. *"The tempter came to him and said, 'If you are the Son of God, tell these stones to become bread.'"* No doubt Jesus was hungry after feasting for several days. I am sure the thought of His hunger was constantly on His mind. I believe that there are many occasions when we do not even hear the voice of the Spirit of God because the sound of our own lusts and desires drown it out.

It is interesting that Satan did not suggest for Jesus to create a horse to ride up the mountain and carry Him back home. He did not suggest for Him to call down a host of angels to sing for Him and help get His mind off His hunger. No, Satan, did what he does best. He attacked Him through His feelings, cravings, and weakness.

Our feelings can be a major distraction away from the leadership of the Holy Spirit. Paul explains in Galatians 5 and writes, *"For the sinful nature desires what is contrary to the Spirit, and the Spirit what is contrary to the sinful nature. They are in conflict with each other, so that you do not do what you want."* If this is true, then we can assume that our natural inclination is seldom going to be to follow the Spirit of God. Even if I want to do what God wants, according to Paul, my physical desires are going to fight against my spirit and regularly win out. I think the key to offsetting this natural order of things is to prepare ourselves to learn to pay more attention to what the Spirit of God says than what we desire and feel. Paul, in 1 Corinthians 2, teaches us how to do just that.

In 1 Corinthians 2: 13-16, Paul writes, *"13 This is what we speak, not in words taught us by human wisdom but in words taught by the Spirit, expressing spiritual truths in spiritual words. 14 The man without the Spirit does not accept the things that come from the Spirit of God, for they are foolishness to him, and he cannot understand them, because they are spiritually discerned. 15 The spiritual man makes judgments about all things, but he himself is not subject to any man's judgment: 16 'For who has known the mind of the Lord that he may instruct him?' But we have the mind of Christ."* The spiritual man and woman make decisions based on guidance and leadership by the Holy Spirit. They are instructed by the Spirit. As a result, they begin to live daily with the mind of Christ. It is the same mind that thought to say to the tempter, *"It is written: 'Man does not live on bread alone, but on every word that comes from the mouth of God.'"*

One of the necessities for Spirit-led living is a working knowledge of the Scriptures. There are promises within the Word of God we can call into action when we are tempted. The promises of God are sure. Even though we are often pushed around by our feelings and preferences, the Word of God will keep us focused on what will truly bring blessings into our lives. Satan bargains with what isn't his to bargain with.

In Matthew 4 Satan tries to make the bread of life give up his inheritance for something He was just laying aside for a season. Later in the account of Christ's temptation, Satan offered Him Lordship, a position which was already His. The point I am trying to make is that our lust always bargains with us to follow it with what is ours anyway. A man, falling to the temptation to cheat on his wife, finds out afterwards that what He was offered was not even as good as what he had.

Hendriksen writes this about the third temptation of Christ, "On the surface it may therefore seem as if the third temptation was for Christ no temptation at all. Jesus knew that the devil was lying; that is, that the prince of evil had no enchanting kingdoms to give away."[5] If we continue to live our lives led by our feelings we will find ourselves wanting and lacking in the end. It is the Spirit who leads us to true fulfillment. The Spirit of God knows our past, present, and future and is working to bring to pass our destiny. In 1 Corinthians 2:10,

---

[5] William Hendriksen, "Matthew," *New Testament Commentary* (Grand rapids, MI: Baker 1973) 233.

Paul claims that "The Spirit searches all things, even the deep things of God." I believe there are some amazing things God has planned for each of us that our feelings have no clue about. I do not want to give in to temptation, hunger, fatigue, depression, or lust just moments before a major breakthrough in my life. I am sure you do not want that in your life.

The key is being led by the Spirit of God because the Spirit of God searches even the deep things of God. It may not always feel the best to follow the leading of the Spirit but doing so will always yield the greatest blessings and facilitate you walking in your Destiny now! Paul puts it this way in 1 Corinthians 2:9, *"However, as it is written: 'No eye has seen, no ear has heard, no mind has conceived what God has prepared for those who love him.'"*

Professor Mathew has put into words a one-of-a-kind manual for successful ministry. I have purchased copies of his book, *Spirit-Led Ministry In The 21st Century*, for each member of my leadership team. My plan is to use Mathew's book to illustrate the multifaceted options for implementing the leadership of the Holy Spirit into every area of ministry.

I love the book. There seems to be too few books available that are scholarly and emphasize the power and work of the Holy Spirit. The book is such a wonderful tool for pastors to use to teach his or her leadership team. There are sections on pastoral care, children's ministry, praise ministry, women's ministry, church administration, and so much more.

    I believe that the influence and leadership of the Holy Spirit in my preaching makes all the difference in the world. I especially loved how Mathew's presupposition about the purpose of preaching centered on evangelism. He writes, "Biblical preaching is still converting the world and confounding the wise."[6] There are many challenges of ministry in this new century and Mathew has exposed some of the very struggles I have encountered while trying to lead my congregation into the 21st Century. Mathew dedicates portions of the book to some vital aspects of church ministry and gives specialized attention to explaining some important details about each of them.

The name of our church's ministry is Destiny NOW and I especially liked how the author expressed his purpose for writing the

---

[6]Thompson K. Mathew, 153.

book. Mathew states, "I have attempted to present a theology of ministry that is faithful to the Bible and the history of the Church and that takes into account the work of the Holy Spirit NOW."[7] This one statement is revolutionary in my opinion. My frequent struggle in ministry has to do with encouraging the people of God to move with Him and to remain in His glory. Henry Blackaby writes, "Find out where God is at work and join him there."[8] Thompson K.

---

[7] Thompson K. Mathew, x.

[8] Henry Blackaby, *Experiencing God*, Baptist Press (17 May 2005).

Mathew has produced a theology of ministry I can use.

Study can only take me so far when it comes to preaching. I depend greatly on the unction and illumination of the Holy Spirit. I respect Mathew for pointing out that much preaching done today is prefaced with not much, if any, diligent study of the word of God. Simply depending on God to bring to mind what is to be spoken is not enough to be considered spirit-led preaching and teaching. Holy Spirit empowered preaching and teaching is what I believe is desperately needed today and there is nothing more powerful that a prepared preacher saturated in the anointing of the Holy Spirit.

One of my favorite aspects of Mathew's book is the section on divine healing. Healing is an important part of my ministry. It should be a central part of everyone's ministry. Healing happens during miraculous displays but also as part of a process of wholeness. Mathew states, "Healing has been part of the gospel from the very beginning."[9] When my wife was a young teenager she was diagnosed with a rare blood disease. Several doctors worked diligently to appropriately prescribe treatment. However,

---

[9]Thompson K. Mathew, 197.

the medications they prescribed for her were not working.

On a Sunday morning she was watching Oral Roberts on television and Pastor Roberts called for someone watching who had been recently diagnosed with a blood disease to trace their hand on a sheet of paper and write their prayer request in the palm. He proceeded then to say that God was going to do a work of healing. Without telling her parents she stopped taking her medication and immediately began to show signs of recovery. After a few weeks her father discovered she had stopped taking her medicine and rushed her back to the hospital. The doctors found no trace of the blood disease.

My wife and I too, as does Professor Mathew, believe that the Holy Spirit is at work today as He was in the first century. We endeavor to lead our congregation into the fullness of God's Spirit. In addition, we constantly encourage them to grow in their willingness to be led by the Holy Spirit. We have seen too many pastors who manage their congregations instead of leading them. As a result, we try to lead the people of God He has given us to shepherd into constant encounters with God, regular walks of faith, and anointing of the Holy Spirit.

Thompson K. Mathew writes, "The size of a church should not determine the quality of its ministry."[10] Perhaps the most enlightening of all lessons I have learned from Mathew's book is that quality matters too. In response to his reminder that there has to be care for the congregation beyond the hierarchy, I have endeavored to begin a thorough evaluation of each ministry within the church to assure quality care is being given to God's people. Professor Mathew's book is a much needed

---

[10]Thompson K. Mathew, 231.

resource for pastors and ministers who wish to be Spirit-Led and relevant in the 21st Century. The practical and scholarly way the book is presented makes it much more than a theology of the church. It is a ministry manual for a new millennia.

CHAPTER 2

Spirit-Led Thinking in the 21st Century

In Romans 8:5-11, Paul writes, "*5 Those who live according to the sinful nature have their minds set on what that nature desires; but those who live in accordance with the Spirit have their minds set on what the Spirit desires. 6 The mind of sinful man is death, but the mind controlled by the Spirit is life and peace; 7 the sinful mind is hostile to God. It does not submit to God's law, nor can it do so.
8 Those controlled by the sinful nature cannot please God. 9 You, however, are controlled not by the sinful nature but by the Spirit, if the Spirit of God lives in you. And if anyone does not have the Spirit of Christ, he does not belong to*

Christ. 10 But if Christ is in you, your body is dead because of sin, yet your spirit is alive because of righteousness.

11 And if the Spirit of him who raised Jesus from the dead is living in you, he who raised Christ from the dead will also give life to your mortal bodies through his Spirit, who lives in you."

    Spirit-led thinking begins with having our minds renewed. To take it a step forward we could say that Spirit-led thinking requires our thinking to be controlled by the Holy Spirit. Considering that we belong to God anyway, it does not seem too farfetched to at least consider giving our thoughts over to the leadership of the Spirit.

There once lived a boy named Joseph who crafted a toy sailboat out of a piece of wood. Joseph loved the little sailboat he made with his own two hands. He would often sail the boat in the creek next to his house and run beside it along the river bank. One day, the water in the creek was flowing unusually rapid. Joseph had to run to keep up with his little sailboat. Soon, to his disappointment, the little wooden sailboat sailed downstream and out of sight.

It wasn't long after losing the toy that Joseph forgot all about his little toy sailboat. Then one day, while walking along the sidewalk in the small town near where he lived, Joseph noticed his little toy sailboat in the window of the local thrift store. Immediately Joseph went inside to the sales clerk to reclaim his creation. The store manager told him that he had purchased the toy from someone who had found it and brought it into the store. The clerk told Joseph that if he wanted his boat back he would have to buy it.

With only a few dollars and some change in his pocket, Joseph spent all he had to purchase back the little toy sailboat he had made by with his own hands. After leaving the store and walking out onto the sidewalk, Joseph stopped, looked at the toy in his hand, and said to it, "little sailboat, you are twice mine. I made you and then I bought you." God made each of us and through His Son, Jesus, who has paid for, in His own body, the remission of our sins, bought us. We are twice God's.

Our life belongs to God and so it should be lived for God. God has made and paid for our life and has the right to our dedicated service. The new life we receive in Christ is a precious gift and is very valuable in the work of the Lord. Living our Christian life without Christian Service is a terrible waste. God rewards those who serve him. Paul admonishes his readers, in Romans 12: 1-2, and writes, *"I urge you therefore, brethren, by the mercies of God, to present your bodies a living and holy sacrifice, acceptable to God, [which is] your spiritual service of worship. And do not be conformed to this world, but be transformed by the renewing of your mind, that you may prove what the will of God is, that which is good and acceptable and perfect."* Jesus made and paid for our lives. Therefore, as Paul points out, we should be willing to sacrifice a part of our life to Christian Service.

It seems reasonable, according to Paul, for Christians to present their bodies to God for service. A life lived for God is a life well lived. According to Paul, our motivation for service needs to be nothing more than the fact that Jesus has sacrificed so much for us and deserves for us to be willing to do the same for each other. "The original text does not have the word, "body," but instead has "your members."[11] Each aspect of our life can be used in Christian Service to some capacity.

God sent Jesus as a sacrifice for sin and He, indeed, gave his body to be offered up on the cross. In addition, He served others with his ability to heal, comfort, provide, deliver, and council. All these various facets of Jesus' life, in addition to his body, were used sacrificially in service to the Father. He expects believers to follow His example and be willing to do for others what He was so willing to do for us. There is much good each of us can accomplish

---

[11]Everett F. Harrison, "Romans," *The Expositor's Bible Commentary,* vol. 10 ed. Frank E. Gaebelein. (Zondervan, Grand Rapids, 1976), 127.

if we live our life out of a motivation to serve others.

Jesus served others. We too should live to serve others. Jesus had the right to live like a king in the world he created, yet when He came to earth he lived as a humble servant. This is why Paul urges the Roman believers to see their sacrifice and servitude as an act of worship. Jesus had every right to be worshipped, yet he worshipped. God had the right to condemn man yet He willingly served man. Although His right was King, His role was servant.

Christians may be, according to Paul, part of the royal priesthood of God, yet they are encouraged to assume the role of servant. Paul writes, *"present your bodies a living and holy sacrifice, acceptable to God."* This section of Romans is a theological treatise devoted to the praxis of Christian Service. Paul reminds the Romans that God's grace should stimulate sacrificial giving of oneself in service to God.[12] There is blessing for personal sacrifice. Luke writes, in Luke 18: 29-30, *"And He said to them, 'Truly, I say to you, there is no one who*

---

[12]D.A. Carson. Douglas J. Moo, and Leon Morris, "Romans," *An Introduction to the New Testament*, (Zondervan, Grand Rapids, 1992). 241.

has left house or wife or brothers or parents or children, for the sake of the kingdom of God, 30 who shall not receive many times as much at this time and in the age to come, eternal life." A life lived for self is a life lost.

True Christians think differently than the world. Paul, in verse 2, writes; "And do not be conformed to this world, but be transformed by the renewing of your mind, that you may prove what the will of God is, that which is good and acceptable and perfect." It sounds like Paul is saying that the opposite of being conformed to this world is having a renewed mind. Like Christ, Christians have a giving attitude. Paul is admonishing his readers to share the same sacrificial and beneficent attitude as Christ. Jesus lived His life in a way that validated His claim to be "busy about His Father's business." In Luke 17:33, Jesus says, *"Whoever tries to keep his life will lose it, and whoever loses his life will preserve it."* A life lived for self is a life lost.

Christians are frequently tempted to be self-centered. Even in our prayer life we too often pray selfish prayers instead of interceding for others. "Research has shown that the average Christian prays less than four minutes a day, including meal times."[13] If most Christians pray for personal needs more than the needs of others, this statistic shows little or no time is spend interceding for others.

Christians are often selfish with our giving. Christians often seem to have just enough money to provide for their own "perceived" needs. Perceived needs may be things one thinks one needs but actually does not. Truly we could all do without a little for the sake of giving to others. There is great blessing in praying for others and giving to God and to

---

[13]Dan Britts, "Lord, Teach Us to Pray," *Davis Chinese Christian Church,* Davis, CA. http://d-ccc.org/sermons /db010503.htm. (10 November 2010).

others. As Paul writes, *"that you may prove what the will of God is."* The blessed life which follows the life of servitude proves that it works and demonstrates that a life is a terrible thing to waste.

One of the most wasteful aspects of a life lived selfishly is absence of the perfection process. The perfecting of the saints involves having a renewed mind which regularly thinks of others. It involves learning how to think like Christ thinks. Christ thought of others ahead of himself and God blessed Him for it. The Christian life is a life of service and a life of service will bring blessings to oneself and others.

I would like to encourage each of you to change your thinking today to a more progressive way of thinking about service to others and giving to God. You have one life and your life would be a terrible thing to waste.

CHAPTER 3

Spiritual Leadership "Shepherds"

In Ephesians 4: 11-13, the Bible says, *"11 It was he who gave some to be apostles, some to be prophets, some to be evangelists, and some to be pastors and teachers, 12 to prepare God's people for works of service, so that the body of Christ may be built up 13 until we all reach unity in the faith and in the knowledge of the Son of God and become mature, attaining to the whole measure of the fullness of Christ."*

"Pastor," is one of the gifts given by the ascended Jesus to equip the church to do the work of ministry. "The gifts He gave to His own were secured consequent to His victory over death to enable them to also be victorious while carrying on His work on earth and hereafter."[14] Because the Pastor of the local congregation is a gift from God, he or she should be greatly appreciated.

In Ephesians 4: 11-12, Paul shows that pastors are included in the 5-fold equipping gifts God gave to the body of Christ following Jesus' death, burial, resurrection, and ascension. Later in verse 13, he includes pastors by using the word "all." Although

---

[14]Spiros Zodhiates, "Notes on Ephesians 4," in *Hebrew-Greek Key Word Study Bible*, NASB (Chattanooga, TN, AMG Publishers 1990). 1565.

pastors are God's gift to the church, they too are on a journey to reach unity in the faith and in the knowledge of the Son of God and become mature, attaining to the whole measure of the fullness of Christ.

    The book of Ephesians is one of Paul's five "Prison Epistles."[15] Throughout the epistle, Paul shows that the church is the body of Christ. Jesus is the head of the body and he resides in heaven while the church exists on earth as the body of Christ.

---

    [15]Spiros Zodhiates, "Notes on Ephesians," in *Hebrew-Greek Key Word Study Bible*, NASB (Chattanooga, TN, AMG Publishers 1990).1560.

Paul uses several figures of speech to describe the body of Christ. Paul points out that the Church is like a body with Christ as the head and the Church is like a building with Christ as the cornerstone and the Church is like a wife with Christ as the husband.

The purpose of the selected text seems to be revealed in verse 13 when Paul mentions the "fullness of Christ." This is the same phrase Paul uses in the concluding verse of the very first chapter. "The church, which is the body of Christ, is described in Ephesians 4:23 as *'the fullness of Him who fills everything in every* way.'"[16] There is a special place for pastors in the body of Christ, as there is for apostles, prophets, evangelists, and teachers.

"After his short visit to Palestine and Syria in the Spring of A.D. 52, Paul made his way back to Ephesus."[17] The Apostle Paul had, in addition to some opportunities to share the gospel to the Ephesians, his share of opposition. According to Paul in 1 Corinthians

---

[16]Skevington A. Wood, *Ephesians through Philemon*. The Expositor's Bible Commentary. Vol. 11. Frank E. Gaebelein, ed. (Grand Rapids: MI: Zondervan) 31.

[17]F.F. Bruce, Ephesus: "Open Door and Many Adversaries," in *Paul: Apostle of the Heart Set Free*. (Grand Rapids, MI: Eerdmans Publishing, 1977) 286.

16:9, *"There were many adversaries."* He wrote his epistle to the Ephesians while under house detention in Rome.[18]

Paul wrote Ephesians to declare the gospel of Jesus Christ. Paul meant the Ephesians letter to be read by everyone who had the opportunity. In his letter to the Ephesians, "Paul did not deal with particular issues, as in Colossians and in much of his

---

[18]Skevington A. Wood, *Ephesians through Philemon*. The Expositor's Bible Commentary. Vol. 11. Frank E. Gaebelein, ed. (Grand Rapids: MI: Zondervan) 16.

other correspondence, but with the implications of the gospel."[19]

Ephesus was a thriving city. It was the capital of the province of Asia and the leading city of Asia Minor, where the church grew very rapidly.[20] There were both Jews and Gentiles living in Ephesus. The population of the city made it a perfect focus for mass evangelization by Paul and his cohort.

In Ephesians 4:12, Paul gives the purpose of pastors, along with apostles,

---

[19]Skevington A. Wood, 16.

[20]Paul Trebilco, "The Early Christians in Ephesus, from Paul to Ignatius."

prophets, evangelists, and teachers. Paul points out that the purpose of local church pastors is *"to prepare God's people for works of service, so that the body of Christ may be built up."* Pastors are God's gift to the body of Christ. However, it should be noted that the body is Christ's body. Therefore, the words of service produced through the body should be Christ-centered.

There is an obvious ecclesiological theme permeating Ephesians 4: 11-13. Although Paul was writing to church leaders in the first century, his theology can and should be applied today. Lewis Sperry Chafer refers to the gifts mentioned in verse 11 of Ephesians 4 as "abiding ministry gifts."[21] The pastor of the local church is one of the abiding ministry gifts which God gives the church. As seen in Ephesians 4, "Office was by appointment, ministry was by gift of the Spirit."[22]

Church members and attendees should consider pastors as gifts from God. Thompson K. Mathew states that, "Donald E. Messer believes that many people consider ministers

---

[21]Lewis S. Chafer, "Ecclesiology: The Church As An Organism," in *Chafer Systematic Theology*, Vol. 4. (Dallas, TX: Dallas Seminary Press, 1948, Revised, 1975) 152.

[22]Lewis S. Chafer, 152.

as hired hands."[23] The church needs to recognize pastors as one of the fivefold ministry gifts Jesus gave to the church. "Nothing can change the fact that pastors are ministry gifts. It is one of the fivefold ascension-gift ministries given by Christ to the Church."[24] Christianity is based on the love shown by Him to the world when He gave the world His Son, Jesus. The Church needs to value all of the gifts of God, including pastors. When members

---

[23]Thompson K. Mathew, *Challenges Of The New Century*, in "Spirit-Led Ministry in the 21st Century." (Xulon Press, 2004) 67.

[24]Kevin J. Conner, *The Church in the New Testament*, (Portland OR: City Bible Publishing, 1982). 175.

and attendees begin to value the pastor as a gift from God, pastors and their ministries will cease to suffer from being perceived through stereotypical images.

The major theme of Paul's letter to the Ephesians is that the church is the body of Christ. The key thought in Ephesians 4:11-13 is that the body has individual parts that must operate as a unit. "God's plan is to bring all believers together with Christ as the head."[25] The Apostle Paul's authorship of Ephesians is

---

[25]Notes on Ephesians, Hebrew-Greek Key Word Study Bible-NIV. Edited by Spiros Zodhiates and warren Baker. (Chattanooga, TN: AMG International, 1996) 1368.

agreed upon by most scholars. "The epistle to the Ephesians has been called the divinest composition of man, the distilled essence of the Christian religion, the most authoritative and most consummate compendium of the Christian faith, full to the brim with thoughts and doctrines sublime and momentous."[26] Harold Hoehner divides the book of Ephesians into

---

[26]William Hendriksen, *Exposition of Ephesians* in "New Testament Commentary-Galatians, Ephesians, Philippians, Colossians, and Philemon." (Grand Rapids, MI: Baker Academic, 2007) 32.

two main sections, "The Calling of the Church and The Conduct of the Church."[27]

In Ephesians 4: 11-13, Paul is exhorting the readers to conduct themselves in a unified way and he goes on to explain to them precisely how to walk in unity. The theme of unity in this passage fits the overall theme of the chapter. Paul begins chapter 4 with an exhortation to humility, gentleness, patience and love. Chrysostom writes, concerning this unifying love to which Paul refers, that "the love

---

[27]Harold W. Hoehner, "Ephesians." *The Bible Knowledge Commentary-New Testament Edition*. Edited byJohn F. Walvoord and Roy B Zuck. (USA, Canada, England: Victor Books, 1983.) 614.

Paul requires of us is no common love, but that which cements us together, and makes us cleave inseparably to one another, and effects as great and as perfect a union as though it were between limb and limb."[28]

The theme of the text is unity in the body as a result of love and considering your brother or sister ahead of yourself. Paul, in Ephesians 4:4-6 writes, *"There is one body and one Spirit-- just as you were called to one hope when you were called - 5 one Lord, one faith, one*

---

[28]John Chrysostom, *Nicene and Post-Nicene Fathers*. Vol. 13. Edited by Philip Schaff. (Peabody Mass: Hendrickson, 2004) 102.

baptism; 6 one God and Father of all, who is over all and through all and in all." After emphasizing the oneness and unity of the body, Paul begins Ephesians 4:7 with the word, "But." "But" is a conjunction in verse 7.

A conjunction is "any member of a small class of words distinguished in many languages by their function as connectors between words, phrases, clauses, or sentences, as *and, because, but, however.*"[29] *"But,"* is connected to the previous section and

---

[29]Merriam-Webster, "*Conjunction*," Webster's Ninth New collegiate Dictionary, (Springfield, Mass: Merriam-Webster Publishing, 1987), 277.

tied to the forgoing theme. *"But," is* δέ in the Greek and is a primary particle that means "moreover."[30] Paul is stressing that although every Christian is a part of the "one" body of Christ, each member of the body has been given grace proportionately. Prior to verse 7, Paul has been focusing on the whole. Now, however, he draws attention to the individual. Every member of the body of Christ shares a measure of God's grace.

---

[30]Strongs G1161, "de" in *Blue Letter Bible* 1996-2010 (6 September 2009) < http://ww.blueletterbible.org/lang /lexicon/lexicon.cfm? (9 September 2010).

"This is equipping grace rather than saving grace that Paul describes."[31] The offices presented by Paul in Ephesians 11 may very well be referred to as "equipping ministry gifts." Paul, in verse 12, declares the purpose of these individuals is for the "preparing of God's people for works of service." According to Paul, Apostles, Prophets, Evangelists, Pastors, and Teachers are all gifts from God to the church. "Apostles, Prophets, Evangelists, Pastors, and

---

[31]Skevington Wood A., *Ephesians through Philemon*. The Expositor's Bible Commentary. Vol. 11. (Grand Rapids: MI: Zondervan, 1981), 57.

Teachers are part of the spiritual DNA Christ has for the body."[32]

Pastors are a gift from God to the Church and should be treated accordingly. Too frequently pastors are looked upon as employees of the congregation rather than gifted individuals sent from God to lead people. In Ephesians 4: 11-13, Paul indicates that the fivefold ministry gifts were given to the church by Jesus to equip the saints. It is clear from the epistle to the Ephesians that everyone in the body of Christ is special and significant.

---

[32]Doug Beacham, *Introduction* in "Rediscovering the Role of Apostles and Prophets." (Franklin Springs, GA: LifeSprings Resources, 2004), viii.

However, certain people are given certain gifts for God's selected purposes within the congregation. Disunity within the church prevails when there is a misunderstanding of or resistance to the God-ordained leadership structure.

Paul makes it clear in verse 7 that God gives gifts to everyone. Paul includes himself as a recipient by saying, "to each one of us grace has been given." It is not God's intention to leave anyone out when it comes to giving gifts. However, it is Christ Himself who distributes the gifts in the proportion He chooses. It should not be a subject of contention within the church for God to gift some to serve as Apostles, Prophets, Evangelists, Pastors, or Teachers, and not others. Not everyone is called to be a leader. In verse 8, Paul introduces the subject of church leadership into the passage using Jesus as an example.

Paul writes in verse 8, *"When he ascended on high, he led captives in his train and gave gifts to men."* The Greek word in this verse translated, "ascended," is *anabainō*, which means, "to go or come up." [33] Paul is

---

[33]Strongs G305, "*anabainō*" in *Blue Letter Bible* 1996-2010 (6 September 2009).

saying that when Jesus went up, He led the capture. In any battle there must be a distinct battle cry to sound the charge. Without leadership within the local church, there will be little territory captured for the Kingdom of God.

It seems clear that Paul is illustrating a kind of leadership structure in this passage. In addition, he gives the purpose for the ministry gifts given by the resurrected Lord. Paul writes in verse 12 that the purpose of the ministry gifts is "to prepare God's people for works of service, so that the body of Christ may be built up." There are three particulars in verse 12 about pastors, as well as the other four ministry gifts, which illustrate the importance for the congregation to maintain a high regard for the pastor.

The pastor's main responsibility is to labor in the Word of God and prepare God's people. Paul writes again in 1 Timothy 5, that *"The elders who direct the affairs of the church well are worthy of double honor, especially those whose work is preaching and teaching."* Pastors, as God's gift to the church, who perform their duties well, are worthy of twice the honor given to anyone else. Another particular point to ponder is the fact that pastors are given the oversight of God's people. The very fact that God would entrust His people with a pastor merits a significant level of respect for him or her. Finally, pastors have the responsibility of helping to build the body of Christ. As negative as it was for the soldiers to tear the fleshly body of Christ apart at His crucifixion, is how positive it is for pastors to build up the body of Christ.

Just as the theme of the book of Ephesians is the body of Christ Ephesians 4:11-13 centers on God's ministry gifts to the church. Pastors, as one of these five ministry gifts, are valuable to the church and are God's chosen leaders and equippers of the people.

Usually, we value gifts given to us by those who are special in our lives. Pastors, as a special gift from God Himself, should be valued and considered a very special gift to the church.

Beginning in verse 1 of Ephesians 4, Paul emphasizes the importance of particular individuals within the body of Christ. In Ephesians 4: 7-13 Paul writes, *"7 But to each one of us grace was given according to the measure of Christ's gift. 8 Therefore it says, "WHEN HE ASCENDED ON HIGH, HE LED CAPTIVE A HOST OF CAPTIVES, AND HE GAVE GIFTS TO MEN." 9 (Now this* [expression,] "He ascended," what does it mean except that He also had descended into the lower parts of the earth? 10 He who descended is Himself also He who ascended far above all the heavens, that He might fill all things.) 11 And He gave some [as] apostles, and some [as] prophets, and some [as] evangelists, and some [as] pastors and teachers, 12 for the equipping of the saints for the work of service, to the building up of the body of Christ; 13 until we all attain to the unity of the faith, and of the knowledge of the Son of God, to a mature man, to the measure of the stature which belongs to the fullness of Christ."

This passage is an excerpt from a larger section of Ephesians in which Paul is writing about unity.

James Modlish, in his outline of Ephesians 4, titles chapter 4, verses 1-16, "Walking in Unity." "The Spirit was given to Christ without measure, but grace is given to the Christian according to measure…the measure you need."[34] Who is the giver of this grace? These individuals named by Paul in Ephesians 4, are given to the church as "gifts,"

---

[34] James Modlish, "Ephesians Four," The Bible Study Page, 20 October 2010 http://www.thebiblestudypage.com/eph_4.shtml. (15 November 2010).

and not just gifts but "grace gifts." "Grace," in Ephesians 4:7, is "χά ρις -Charis," and is "a favor done without expectation of return; absolute freeness of the lovingkindness of God to men finding its only motive in the bounty and free heartedness[35] of the giver."[36] In verse 8, "gifts," is "δό μα-Doma." According to Freidrich, "In Ephesians 4: 7-11, Christ is described as the one who dispenses in fullness the gifts of

---

[35]"Gifts," blueletterbible.org Lexicon, http://www.blueletterbible.org/Bible.cfm?b=Eph&c=4&t= NASB#conc/8 (14 November 2010).

[36]Charis, "Lexical Aids to the New Testament," *Hebrew-Greek Key Word Study Bible*, ed., Spiros Zodhiates, (Chattanooga, TN., AMG Publishers, 1990) 1887.

grace. He is this because He has achieved dominion over all powers, both the lowest and the highest."[37] One of the gifts He dispenses to the church is "pastors." "Pastors," in verse 11, is ποιμήν -Poimen, which means shepherd.[38] From the very beginning of the epistle, Paul highlights the significance of each individual believer in the body of Christ.

Beginning in verse 1 of Chapter 4, Paul emphasizes the importance of particular

---

[37]"πληρόω," "Theological Dictionary of the New Testament," ed., Gerhard Friedrich, Vol. 6 (Grand Rapids, MI., Eerdmans 1968) 291.

[38]Poimen, "Lexical Aids to the New Testament," *Hebrew-Greek Key Word Study Bible*, ed., Spiros Zodhiates, (Chattanooga, TN., AMG Publishers, 1990) 1869.

individuals within the body. Ephesians 4: 7-13 deals with the body ministry gifts. An outline of the passage would include three main points, "The giving of all things (v.7-9)," "The Filling of all things (10-11)," and "The attainment of all things (12-13)." Following the theme of unity he started in chapter 1, Paul endeavors to highlight the fact that even though there are various offices in the church, everyone is important.

Given to the church as gifts are apostles, prophets, evangelists, pastors and teachers. Although Paul does not differentiate which offices are given the primary responsibility of equipping the saints, various other biblical passages, which will be look at later, bear out the claim that pastors and teachers are given that role in the local church. As gifts from God, the individuals who hold each of these offices should be honored. "Pastors are a gift from God and should be treated as such by those in the local congregation." A thorough analysis of the text will show this to be true.

One comparison of various Greek texts reveal that Lachmann, Tischendorf, Wordsworth, and Nestle-Aland all omit "and" before "gave" and render "he gave" in 4:8. Griesbach, Lachmann, Tischendorf, Tregelles,

Alford, Wordsworth, Westcott & Holt, and Nestle-Aland all omit "first" after "descended" in 4:9. Wordsworth, and Nestle-Aland all omit "parts" after "lower" in 4:9.[39] However, there are few places in the book of Ephesians where any textual uncertainty is found.[40] Carson, Moo, and Morris state that "Apart from the destination in the opening sentence, we can

---

[39] Michael D. Marlowe, "An English Guide to the Various Readings of the Greek New Testament." http://www.bible-researcher.com/ephesians.html (15 November 2010).

[40] A. Skevington Wood, "Ephesians through Philemon," in *The Expositor's Bible Commentary*, vol.11. ed., Frank E.Gaebelein, (Grand Rapids: Zondervan, 1981)20.

say that we are not in real doubt about anything substantial in the letter."[41] Paul's reference in verse 8, however, gives a biblical quotation which is not without its difficulties. The NASB, NIV, and many other translations say, "He gave gifts to men." However, the Aramaic Targum on the Psalter and the Syriac Peshitta both read, "Thou has given gifts to men."[42] Its seems that the best variant to use in a formal translation is what the NASB and NIV uses. Paul's intention was to fit the traditional oral translation of an

---

[41] D.A. Carson, Douglas J. Moo, Leon Morris, "Ephesians," in *An Introduction to the New Testament* (Grand Rapids, Zondervan 1992). 312.

[42] A. Skevington Wood, 57.

early psalm into the context of his point in the passage. A closer look at linguistics will add a little more light on translation.

Is Paul saying God has given these gifts in the past only or does He continue to give them? Coffman points out that there are two pairs of offices in view in Ephesians 4:11: apostles and prophets, and evangelists and pastor-teachers. Coffman writes, "As Bruce observed, the first pair were effective in the founding of the church, and the second pair are required in all generations."[43]

---

[43] James Burton Coffman, "Commentary on Ephesians 4," (15 November 2010).

In both verses 8 and 11, Paul uses the word "gave" to indicate the giving of these gifts. "Gave" in both verses is δίδωμι –didōmi which is a prolonged form of a primary verb.[44] The tense of the word "gave" in both verse 8 and 11 is similar to that used in Exodus 2:21 when Reuel gave his daughter to Moses for a wife. She was not meant to be a gift that was taken back or temporary. Mackay writes, "No passage is more crucial than this for the welfare and mission of the Christian Church

---

[44]"δίδωμι didōmi"http://www.blueletterbible.org/lang/lexicon/lexicon.cfm?Strongs=G1325&t=NASB (15 November 2010).

today."[45] Although the continuation of at least the second list of gifts from verse 11 in the church is not widely disputed, a historical analysis of Ephesians shows that authorship of the epistle is up for debate.

Pauline authorship of Ephesians is widely accepted. However, valid scholarship exists to reinforce the claim that Paul is not the actual author of the book of Ephesians. "The American scholar E.J. Goodspeed theorized that an admirer of Paul wrote Ephesians toward

---

[45]John A. Mackay, "The Fullness of Christ" in *God's Order-The Ephesians Letter and This Present Time* (New York, NY: McMillan Company, 1953) 149.

the end of the first century. Goodspeed went so far as to suggest that the admirer was Onesimus, the converted slave about whom Paul wrote to Philemon."[46] "Schleiermacher suggested that Ephesians may have been commissioned by Paul but composed by Tychicus."[47] Of course, the question of authorship attributes to the question of when Ephesians was actually written. Those who attribute it to a disciple of Paul late in the first

---

[46] Robert H. Gundry, "The Prison Epistles of Paul," in *A Survey of the New Testament* (Grand Rapids, MI: Zondervan, 1981) 294.

[47] Friedrick D. E. Schleiermacher, "Einleitung in das Neue Testament," in *Sammtliche Werke*, ed. G. Wolde (Berlin: G. Reimer, 1845), 1:165, 166.

century consider it to have been composed around the year A.D. 90.

If one accepts Pauline authorship, the date then depends on the place of origin and the relevant imprisonment. If written from Ephesus, it may have been written between A.D. 54 and 57. If written from Caesarea, the date falls between A.D. 59 and 61.[48]

The epistle to the Ephesians was a letter meant for general circulation in the setting of life or "Sitz im Leben" of that day. It was sent to

---

[48]A Skevington Wood, "Ephesians," in *The Expositor's Bible Commentary*, ed., Vol., 11 Frank E. Gaebelein (Grand Rapids, MI: Zondervan, 1981) 15.

Ephesus and to all the churches founded as a result of the mission there throughout the Asian Province. The hand of God was in Paul's writing of Ephesians. Unlike some of Paul's other writings, his letter to the Ephesians was encouraging and not so theological. This was a much needed attribute of the epistle considering Ephesus was an epicenter for the learning and writing of magical arts.[49] It was a wonderful contribution to the Christian culture of Ephesians to have this letter in a time when pagan worship was prevalent. Arnobius speaks

---

[49]F.F. Bruce, "Ephesus: Open Door and Many Adversaries," in *Paul Apostle of the Heart Set Free*, (Grand Rapids: Eerdmans 1977) 291.

of the temple of Diana falling. This occasion, and others like it, may or may not have influenced the religion and culture of Ephesus.

There was obviously some religious tolerance by the government in Ephesus as recorded by Josephus. The decree of the Ephesians was made by the people for the purpose of securing permission to worship on the Sabbath day, as they had historically done. Josephus declares that "It was decreed by the senate and people that in this affair that concerned the Romans, no one of them should be hindered from keeping the Sabbath day, nor be fined for doing so, but that they may be allowed to do all things according to their laws."[50] Perhaps the condition of the religious culture of Ephesians at that time prompted Paul to write in the literary style in which he chose to write the epistle.

George Barlow states what many sources point out, that in the most ancient copies of the Scriptures, the words "at Ephesus," in verse 1, are missing.[51] The general consensus among scholars is that the letter to the Ephesians was

---

[50]Flavius Josephus, "The Antiquities of the Jews," in *The Works of Josephus*, Book 14, Chapter 10, translated, William Whiston (Peabody, MA: Hendrickson) 382.

[51]George Barlow, "The Epistle To The Ephesians," in *The Preacher's Homiletic Commentary*, vol. 28 (Grand Rapids, MI: Baker, 1996) 123.

actually written to several churches in the area of Ephesus. Ephesians is written in the "epistle style" of Paul's other letters. The difference, however, between Ephesians and Paul's other letters is the content and mood. Carson, Moo, and Morris claim that "Pauline features abound. The structure is like that of the undisputed epistles, and there is a good deal of Pauline language, including words that occur in this letter and the undisputed writings of Paul but nowhere else in the New Testament."[52]

---

[52]D.A. Carson, Douglas J. Moo, Leon Morris, "Ephesians," in *An Introduction to the New Testament* (Grand Rapids, MI: Zondervan, 1992.) 306.

Ephesians fits the description of an epistle. In keeping with the characteristics of the genre of epistle, Ephesians is filled with detailed truth and careful shades of meaning. According to Greidanus, Ephesians is one of the six tractate-type letters.[53] Paul's letter to the Ephesians was intended to be more than strictly a pastoral response to a specific set of issues arising in certain places. The form of the epistle is unique and characteristic of all of Paul's letters. The standard form of the epistles

---

[53]Sidney Greidanus, "Preaching Epistles," in *The Modern Preacher and the Ancient Text-Interpreting and Preaching Biblical Literature* (Grand Rapids, MI: Eerdmans, 1988) 314-315.

consists of three parts, "An introduction, prescript, or salutation, the body or text of the letter, and a conclusion."[54] Although possibly less theological than some of Paul's other epistles, there are some theological lessons to be interpreted from the epistle to the Ephesians.

Due to the variety of religions prominent in and around Ephesus, there was disunity within many churches. However, a strong pursuit for unity existed among many Christians and religious individuals at this time. Paul was

---

[54]Sidney Greidanus, 315.

able to demonstrate that their almost obsessive search for unity finds its ultimate goal only in Christ. One of the ways Ephesians 4 promotes unity is by confirming that church leadership is a gift from God. Paul seemed to want his readers to fall in line under God ordained leadership.

The ecclesiological leadership structure outlined in Ephesians 4:11, at least in Paul's mind, was set up by God to promote unity within the church. Change, however, is not always easy. Neil Ormerod points out that "Ecclesiology is a fundamentally different type of theology from many other more classical theological themes. For example, when we study the doctrine of the Trinity we do not necessarily expect changes to occur in the Trinity itself, even though our understanding of it might grow."[55] It seems, however, that today the set up of ecclesiological leadership structure has moved in a direction away from that which is illustrated in Ephesians 4:7:13.

With democracy being the government of choice, in many countries, over that of kingdom, the understanding of church

---

[55]Neil Ormerod, "On the Divine Institution of the Three-fold Ministry" in *"Ecclesiology"* (Strathfield, AUS Brill Academic Publishers2007).

leadership structure may be misunderstood without some adjustment to present-day ecclesiology. Paul's setting was often a prison cell. Ironically, Paul was jailed for his unwillingness to fall in line with orders of secular leadership that following would have caused him to disobey God. The point is to illustrate that pastors of local congregations are still God's appointed ecclesiological leaders of the church. In addition, pastors are still a gift from God and should be treated accordingly. Church members should understand that it is God's designed ecclesiological order for instruction to come from these offices in Ephesians 4:11.

Augustine emphasized that human direction was not to be despised.[56] Calvin states, "In my opinion, pastors are those who have the charge of a particular flock."[57] Kittel points out that the only time congregational leaders are called ποιμήν shepherds is in

---

[56] Augustine, "On Christian Doctrine," in *City of God* Nicene and Post-Nicene Fathers-1st Edition (Grand rapids, MI: Hendrickson, 2004) 585.

[57] John Calvin, "Epistle to the Ephesians," in *John Calvin's Commentaries* (Grand Rapids, MI: Baker 2003) 280.

Ephesians 4:11.[58] Pastors, as well as each of the other gifts mentioned in Ephesians 4:11 are valuable to the body of Christ. It seems that one of their most important contributions to the church is their leadership, without which unity would be difficult to achieve.

It is obvious that Paul was writing to the Ephesians about the importance of unity and being "in Christ" to find the highest level of it. If adequately applied, the lessons taught in Ephesians 4: 7-13 would revolutionize church

---

[58]"ποιμήν" Theological Dictionary of the New Testament," ed., Kittel, Vol. 5 (Grand Rapids, MI., Eerdmans 1968) 497.

government and change the disorder seen in most congregations to kingdom order. Chafer points out that the abiding ministry gifts are enumerated in Ephesians 4:11 and are not gifts of the Spirit to people, as in 1 Corinthians 12, but gifts of Spirit-gifted people to the church.[59]

As Spirit-gifted people to the church, it stands to reason that pastors would be appreciated by the local congregation. The challenge of this argument is being able to present the Pastor of the church as leader,

---

[59]Lewis Sperry Chaffer, "Ecclesiology: "The Church as an Organism," in *Chaffer Systematic Theology* (Dallas, TX: Dallas Seminary Press, 1980) 152.

while at the same time keeping him or her serving in the role of shepherd/servant. According to Mackay, "No passage in the Bible is more crucial than this passage in Ephesians for the welfare and mission of the Christian Church today."[60]

It seems that Paul, in this passage, was encouraging the believers in and around Ephesus to understand that following the God-given leadership bestowed upon the church by Christ would increase unity. Leaders have no one to lead if there is not anyone willing to

---

[60] John A. Mackay, "The Fullness of Christ," in *The Ephesian Letter and this Present Time* (New York, NY: The Macmillan Company, 1953) 149.

follow. In a situation where several individuals see themselves as the leader of a church, or any organization for that matter, it may be difficult to establish unity. The reason for this difficulty is that people will often choose who they want to follow instead of who God has given them to lead.

Leadership within the church greatly depends on the willingness of the church members to follow the God-appointed man or woman. The research in this chapter has shown that Ephesians 4: 7-13 is a passage written for the purpose of promoting unity with the local congregation and that one of God's strategies for doing so was giving the church gifted leaders. Beginning in verse 1 of Ephesians 4, Paul emphasizes the importance of particular individuals within the body of Christ. Pastors are a gift from God and should be treated as such by the local congregation.

A few unresolved questions about this passage which time and space did not allow expounding on is whether or not pastor and teacher are truly meant to stand alone as one single category of gift. A fair amount of research was done for this paper to support the claim of the thesis statement which focuses on the fact that pastors are a gift from God.

However, more research could be done in an effort to discovery whether or not Paul is emphasizing, in this passage, individual or group leadership within the church.

CHAPTER 4

Powerful Leadership
"The Holy Spirit"

According to Acts 2:42-47, the Baptism of the Holy Ghost affects both the minister and ministry by increasing fruitfulness in the areas of fellowship, performing of miracles, ministering to the needs of the world, and evangelism. Paul writes in Acts 2:42-47, *"They devoted themselves to the apostle's teaching and to fellowship, to the breaking of bread and to prayer. Everyone was filled with awe at the many wonders and signs performed by the apostles. All the believers were together and had everything in common. They sold property and possessions to give to anyone who had need. Every day they continued to meet together in the temple courts. They broke bread in their homes and ate together with glad and sincere hearts, praising God and enjoying the favor of all the people. And the Lord added to their number daily those who were being saved."*

It is obvious from the historical account of this passage that the lives of the followers of Jesus, as well as those of the new converts, had been miraculously altered and empowered subsequent to their experience of Holy Ghost Baptism. The obvious revival of the church, or at least many people, on a brand new spiritual level clearly illustrates that the experience of the Holy Ghost Baptism impacts the level of discipleship, fellowship, personal devotion, miracles, and evangelism in a minister and ministry.

Ministries led by ministers who have received the Holy Ghost Baptism tend to have large numbers in fellowship. Terry Tramel writes, "The distinctive of Pentecostal theology is a companion belief in another experience in the Holy Spirit for the primary purpose of empowerment for mission and ministry.[61] Those ministers and ministries who are

---

[61] Terry Tramel, "The Empowerment of the Holy Spirit," in *The Beauty of The Balance* (Franklin Springs, GA: Lifesprings Resources, 2009), 180.

empowered by the Holy Spirit are especially equipped for missions and ministry and this has been illustrated through the constant growth of Spirit led churches. Testimonies and reports of miracles often come from Pentecostal fellowships. As was the case in Acts 2, so it is within Pentecostal ministries. Ministers and ministries in which Holy Ghost Baptism is sought and experienced receive testimonies of miracles.

Ministers and ministries who have received the Holy Ghost Baptism tend to be geared toward meeting the needs of others. From the start of the church at Pentecost, the experience of Holy Ghost baptism seems to precede tremendous displays of benevolence. In addition, Ministries influenced by a Pentecostal experience are heavily involved in global and domestic evangelism.

When the believers in Acts 2 were baptized they became students of the Apostle's teaching. Christians who study the Word of God live fruitful and productive lives. Paul writes in Hebrews 4:12, *"For the Word of God is alive and active. Sharper than any double-edged sword, it penetrates even to dividing soul and spirit, joints and marrow; it judges the thoughts and attitudes of the heart."* Because the Holy Ghost baptism motivates the believer to study God's Word, the individual who receives Holy Ghost baptism becomes fruitful and productive. Thom Rainer comments on the obvious change in the life of C. Peter Wagner, formerly an "anti-Pentecostal," and writes, "Wagner was healed of a dangerous problem resulting from neck surgery to remove a cyst. The healing took place overnight after Wagner had attended a healing service in Bolivia out of curiosity. Second, the rapid growth of Pentecostalism led the ever pragmatic Wagner to examine some Pentecostal and charismatic churches. His attitude changed dramatically."[62]

C. Peter Wagner is indisputably one of the most recognized advocates of Pentecostal experiences, including Holy Ghost baptism. He is quoted by many other authors across denominational lines. He, along with many other Pentecostal scholars, has written about the enormous growth of Pentecostalism throughout the world. As mentioned above, Wagner's own experience with the Holy Ghost

---

[62]Thom Rainer, "Toward the Twenty-First Century, 1988 to the Future," in *The Book of Church Growth* (Nashville, TN; Broadman and Holman Publishers 1993), 62.

baptism led him to study and teach the fruitfulness and beneficial effects of Holy Ghost baptism to the body of Christ. Perhaps the greatest testimonies which continue to validate the claim that ministers and ministries experiencing the Holy Ghost baptism are fruitful and productive in the areas of fellowship, discipleship, evangelism, and others, is such testimonies as Wagner's.

When the believers in Acts 2 were baptized they gave themselves to prayer. Believers who are baptized in the Holy Ghost have an increased unction to pray. One American Missionary wrote that those who went through the experience of Holy Ghost Baptism felt great pleasure and were usually much changed and full of the spirit of worship, prayer and love.[63] Pentecostals are known as people of prayer. "Prayer, indeed, is foundational to the establishing and sustaining of a healthy, growing congregation."[64] It is evident from the life of Jesus, that God meant

---

[63]Allison Kidd Covington, "Why Pentecostal? A Look at the Phenomenon of Rapid Pentecostal Growth in Latin America," http://inquiry.uark.edu/Covington_Final_for_On-line.pdf (12 December 2009) 11.

[64]Dick Eastmen, "Developing a Prayer Ministry in the Local Church," *The Pentecostal Pastor* Unit 3, Preparing for Revival, ed. Thomas E. Trask, Wayde I. Goodall, and Zenas J. Bicket (Springfield, MI; Gospel Publishing Co., 2000) 237.

for His people to people of prayer. The purpose of Pentecost and the Holy Ghost Baptism has, from the beginning, been for the purpose of empowering ministers and ministries to be fruitful and productive. In fact, the disciples were no doubt engaged in prayer when the Spirit of God descended upon them in the upper room in Jerusalem on the Day of Pentecost. It seems significant to the issue to point out that even Peter's prayer life was illustratively different subsequent to his Holy Ghost Baptism as found in Acts 10:9-13. In this passage, Luke describes the episode and says, "About noon the following day as they were on their journey and approaching the city, Peter went up on the roof to pray. He became hungry and wanted something to eat and while the meal was being prepared, he fell into a trance. He saw heaven opened and something like a large sheet being let down to earth by its four corners. It contained all kinds of four-footed animals, as well as reptiles and birds. Then a voice told him, Get up Peter, kill and eat." Nowhere else in scripture are we told of such an encounter with God during prayer in the life of Peter.

Ever since the Day of Pentecost, ministries led by individuals baptized in the

Holy Ghost have experienced large numbers in fellowship. As a matter of fact, for several decades, Pentecostal ministries have been the fastest growing around the world. For example, in Latin America, beginning early in the twentieth century, the momentum for church growth has been phenomenal. In 1900 there were about fifty thousand Protestants in Latin America, by 2000, there were almost one hundred and fifty million. Most of the growth has come from Pentecostals.[65]

---

[65]Thom Rainer, "Signs and Wonders and Church Growth," in *The Book of Church Growth* (Nashville, TN; Broadman and Holman Publishers 1993), 303.

Pentecostal and charismatic churches see some of the largest numbers of people added to church fellowship annually. C Peter Wagner wrote, "I discovered that in our country (America), the independent charismatic churches were the most rapidly growing segment of Christianity.[66] This is not a surprise to anyone whose life and ministry has been influenced through the experience of Holy Ghost Baptism. It is clear from Acts 2:42 that the Holy Ghost believers of Acts devoted

---

[66]C. Peter Wagner, "The 'Why' of the New Wineskins," *Churchquake*, (Ventura, CA. Regal Publishing, 1999) 11.

themselves to fellowship. Many Pentecostal and charismatic churches are experiencing amazing numerical increase in fellowship while many others are in decline. The fruitfulness of increased fellowship within Pentecostal ministries influenced by the experience of Holy Ghost Baptism is significant. Pentecostalism is one of the world's fastest growing movements.[67] Historically, there has been overwhelming numerical increases in Pentecostal ministries. It seems as though the

---

[67] Jessica Ravitz, Moved by The Spirit: Fastest Growing Pentecostal Church Takes Root in the 'Last Frontier'. *Religion News Blog* (5 May 2006) The Salt Lake Tribune USA

leadership structure of Acts is one which produces fruitfulness and productivity within the Kingdom of God. As fellowship, evangelism, and praise increased, following the Holy Ghost Baptism of the believers in Acts 2, so it is with ministries affected by the empowering of the Spirit. Thom Rainer illustrates Pentecostal leadership in his "Acts 6/7 Legacy Leadership" model and says that breakout churches are normally led by Acts 6/7 leaders.

Acts 6/7 leaders are ministers and ministry leaders who function in the same leadership capacity as those in Acts chapters one through seven.[68] The leaders in Acts were equipped with and empowered by the Holy Spirit. This equipping and empowerment from Holy Ghost baptism produced a fruitful ministry and caused the life of these leaders to be greatly effective. Christianity saw its most vigorous advance around the world in the 19th Century. As a result of the global expansion of Pentecost, the gospel spread vigorously around the world.[69] Fruitfulness and courage to

---

[68]Thom Rainer, *"Breakout Churches"* (Grand Rapids: MI, Zondervan Publishing, 2005) 27.

[69]Gary B. McGee, To the Regions Beyond: "The Global Expansion of Pentecost," in *The Century of the Holy Spirit by Vinson Synan,* (Nashville, TN: Thomas Nelson Publishing, 2001) 69.

minister seems to be the plan and purpose of the Holy Ghost Baptism coming on the Day of Pentecost and continuing throughout the church age. As a result, both minister and ministry have been positively affected.

Perhaps the most overwhelming proof to the claim that many miracles come from Pentecostal fellowships and ministries is that the book of Acts confirms it. During the Day of Pentecost and following, miracles regularly accompanied the followers of Christ. Signs and wonders accompanied the apostle's receipt of the Baptism in the Holy Ghost. Today, miracles are frequently reported among Pentecostals.

Gordon L. Anderson writes, "For Pentecostals, the power given at the baptism of the Holy Spirit allows the believer to minister as Jesus did, and the gifts of the Spirit outlined in 1 Corinthians 12 include miracles."[70]

Acts 2:43 says, "Everyone was filled with awe at the many wonders and signs performed by the apostles." The apostles were empowered by the Holy Spirit. There is a marked difference between the spiritual fruitfulness of their lives prior to Pentecost.

---

[70]Gordon L. Anderson, "Signs and Wonders," in *The Pentecostal Pastor* Unit 3, Preparing for Revival, ed. Thomas E. Trask, Wayde I. Goodall, and Zenas J. Bicket (Springfield, MI; Gospel Publishing Co., 2000) 303.

Although they walked and talked with Jesus, their impact was far greater when they walked with the Holy Spirit. In Matthew 17, a father brought his son to Jesus' disciples who were unable to heal him, yet in Acts 5, the sick were brought to the place where Peter was in hopes that at least his shadow would touch them.

Historically, miracles and healings happened through ministries empowered by Holy Ghost Baptism. This seems clear from the book of Acts. Miracles have happened throughout history and have continued through today. The present day working of miracles is confirmed by several reputable scholars. C.

Samuel Storm says, "The fact that miracles do appear throughout the course of redemptive history, whether sporadically or otherwise, proves that miracles never ceased."[71] Perhaps one of the reasons why miracles seem to be more regularly experienced among Pentecostals is because Pentecostals tend to include their experiences within their hermeneutic process. "The difference between Pentecostals and others is that they use real life experiences with an awareness and

---

[71]C. Samuel Storms, "A Third Wave View," in *Are Miraculous Gifts for Today?* ed., Wayne Grudem and Stanley Gundry. (Grand Rapids: Zondervan 1996) 188.

admission of the fact and a belief that it is an appropriate step in a legitimate hermeneutic. This is connected to their appreciation of the historical narratives and an ecclesiology which sees God functioning throughout the Church Age in the same way as He did in the first century.[72] Miracles, at least in a sense, are part of the whole experience of being a Christian. It seems rational to believe that miracles are more likely to emerge from the lives of people who are apt to consider them possible.

---

[72] Gordon L. Anderson, Pentecostal Hermeneutics Part Two, AG Churches.org, http://agchurches.org/Sitefiles/Default/RSS/IValue/Resources/Holy%20Spirit/Articles/PentecostalHermeneuticsPt2.pdf. (14 December 2009) 5.

According to Acts 2:45, the first Holy Ghost baptized believers was inclined to give to those who were in need. "They sold property and possessions to give to anyone who had need." This act of benevolence is characteristic of ministers and ministries influenced by Holy Ghost baptism. The act of giving is motivated by love and true love can only be known as one knows God. In 1 John 4:21, John says, *"those who love God must love one another."* It is crucial to the body of Christ for ministers and ministries to lead the way in being fruitful in the area of benevolence. Even in the experience of Holy Ghost baptism, Pastors and ministry leaders should lead the way. "Research has shown that no institutional factor is more significant to the overall growth patterns of churches that the effectiveness of pastoral leadership."[73]

Many benevolent ministries in operation around the world are led by Pentecostal organizations or ministers who profess receiving Holy Ghost baptism. At the helm of some of the largest missions efforts in the world are Pentecostal and charismatic

---

[73] Gary L. McIntosh and R. Daniel Reeves, "Life-Giving System 1: Pastor's Spiritual Life," in *Thriving Churches in the Twenty-first Century* (Grand Rapids: Kregel Publications, 2006) 48.

organizations. Of course, this is how it has been since the beginning. "The Azusa Street revival in Los Angeles, California, that began in 1906 and triggered many subsequent revivals around the world is now considered the foremost revival of the century in terms of global impact."[74]

Today there are innumerable amounts of Pentecostal churches and ministries who are leading the way in the work of missions. Taking food and clothing around the globe,

---

[74] Gary B. McGee, "Baptism of the Holy Ghost and Fire! The Revival Legacy of Minnie F. Abrams" *Enrichment Journal* http://enrichmentjournal.ag.org/199803/080_baptism_fire.cfm.(14 December 2009).

Pentecostals, displaying the same fruit shown by the first Pentecostals in Acts 2, are benevolent and self-sacrificing. There is no mistaking the fact that from the Day of Pentecost until now, ministers and ministries influenced by Holy Ghost baptism display love, compassion, benevolence, and generosity.

One of the initial results of Holy Ghost baptism is the unction to witness. Throughout the course of Pentecostal history, even in Acts, a passion to witness has seemed to follow the Pentecostal experience of Holy Ghost baptism. One author put it this way, "Any genuine awakening will have lingering impact."[75] According to Acts 2:47b, one result of the believer's baptism in the Holy Ghost was that the church had souls added to it each day. "And the Lord added to their number daily those who were being saved."

Many strong evangelistic churches are Pentecostal in their experience. Lakewood Church in Houston, TX, for example, is the largest church in America and possesses a

---

[75]Malcolm McDow, "The Southwestern Story," in *Revival* ed. John Avant, Malcolm, Alvin Reid (Nashville,TN: Broadman and Holman Publishers, 1996) 70.

Pentecostal Heritage.[76] Not surprisingly, the tendency for Pentecostal ministries to experience significant evangelistic growth is high. Following the pattern of evangelistic success illustrated in the book of Acts, modern day Pentecostals, influenced by Holy Ghost baptism, reach more people than any other religious sect. A closer look at some of the fastest growing churches in America, as well as many mega churches, will reveal that non-denominational, charismatic/Pentecostal churches have been rapidly growing for

---

[76]Wikipedia, Joel Osteen, (28 November 2009) http://en.wikipedia.org/wiki/Joel_Osteen (14 December 2009).

decades. On such television stations as "TBN" and "Daystar," ministers and ministries in the experience of Holy Ghost Baptism are leading massive world and domestic Missions efforts.

There was a mass evangelistic effort following the Day of Pentecost in Acts 2. There had never been such a display of raw determination on the part of Christ's disciples to reach Jews and Gentiles with the message of salvation and the experience of Holy Ghost baptism. The apostle Peter compared the experience to being drunk with "new wine." He also admonished those who doubted the experience and who were accusing the baptized believers of being drunk, to remember that it was only midday and that it was not time for people to start drinking. Peter went on to explain that the supernatural sight they were experiencing was what Joel had prophesied concerning the outpouring of God's Spirit. Peter, as well as many others, demonstrated a fresh new boldness to witness and share the gospel. In spite of imprisonment, threats and even lashings, the Holy Ghost baptized believers of Acts 2 were strong evangelists. The fruitfulness that comes from experiencing the Holy Ghost baptism is God endued. It was His plan for the experience of Pentecost to become an example of heavenly empowerment so that Christians throughout the ages would follow suit and be bold in their witness. According to one commentary, "The worldwide scope of the Christian witness is anticipated at Pentecost in the roll call of nations in Acts 2:9-11."[77]

Pentecostalism is growing rapidly around the world. In light of Acts 2:42-47, Pentecostal ministries should be growing according to the pattern set forth by the early church. The church in Acts 2 was a Pentecostal church.

---

[77] John B. Polhill, *Acts*, New American Commentary (Nashville; Boardman, 1992), 106

According to Acts 2:42-47,"They devoted themselves to the apostle's teaching and to fellowship, to the breaking of bread and to prayer. Everyone was filled with awe at the many wonders and signs performed by the apostles. All the believers were together and had everything in common. They sold property and possessions to give to anyone who had need. Every day they continued to meet together in the temple courts. They broke bread in their homes and ate together with glad and sincere hearts, praising God and enjoying the favor of all the people. And the Lord added to their number daily those who were being saved."

For the believers in Acts 2:42-47 to demonstrate such faith, service, and benevolence, they had to have had a very unique experience. In a culture where many people lived their lives for themselves, these ministers, filled with the Spirit of God, showed care and compassion to others, even others of another race. The Holy Ghost baptism had impacted many Jews to the point that they were willing to ignore the traditional rule of not eating with Gentiles. Some of the fruitfulness of the Holy Ghost baptism for these new believers was being willing to fellowship with people of a different race. Historically, this has been the case in the lives of those experiencing Holy Ghost Baptism. Vinson Synan, writing about Azusa Street, says "The interracial aspects of Azusa Street were a striking exception to the racism and segregation of the times."[78]

It is interesting to see how churches and ministries with ministers who have been baptized with the Holy Ghost, promote multi-racial and multi-cultural worship. This

---

[78]Vinson Synan, The Pentecostal Century: An Overview in *The Century of the Holy Spirit by Vinson Synan,* (Nashville, TN: Thomas Nelson Publishing, 2001) 5.

ecclesiastical integration seems to be not only biblically but historically Pentecostal. One source says, "To those outside the movement, Pentecostals have always seemed exotic, a strange subculture with weird, even frightening, practices. How then to explain that according to the World Christian Database, it is now the second-largest and fastest-growing Christian group in the world, behind the Catholic Church, with about 580 million followers? Or that formal Episcopalians and contemplative Catholics include Pentecostal practices in their services? Or that nearly every mainline and evangelical denomination has been influenced by

Pentecostal musical styles, as anyone who has been to a contemporary worship service can attest?"[79]

According to Acts 2:42-47, the baptism of the Holy Spirit affects both minister and ministry by increasing fruitfulness in the areas of fellowship, performing of miracles, ministering to the needs of the world, and evangelism.

There is truly a difference between the Pentecostal minister and the ministry of others.

---

[79]Cary McMullen, "Pentecostals Celebrate World's Fastest Growing Religion," The Ledger.com, http://www.theledger.com/article/20060424/NEWS/604240374?Title=Pentecostals-Celebrate-World-s-Fastest-Growing-Religion (14 December 2009).

Pentecostal ministries, led by Holy Ghost baptized ministers are impacting the world on a monumental level. The Universal Church of the Kingdom of God, in Brazil, is led by Edir Macedo, and has been the fastest growing church during the last few years.

It now numbers more than 3 million. In Europe, the three largest churches, manna Church in Lisbon, Portugal, led by Jorge Tadeu, Kinsington Temple in London, pastured by Colin Dye, and Faith Church in Budapest,

Hungary, pastured by Sandor Nemeth, are all led by Holy Ghost filled individuals.[80]

It seems evident from the scriptures, as well as from considerable amounts of resources, that Holy Ghost baptism increases fruitfulness in ministry and in the life of the minister. Since the Day of Pentecost, lives have been empowered through Holy Ghost Baptism. Statistics have proven and continue to show that ministries that are exposed to the power of Pentecost are greatly effective in the

---

[80]C. Peter Wagner, "Protestantism's New Look," *Churchquake*, (Ventura, CA. Regal Publishing, 1999) 47-48.

areas of fellowship, ministry, and evangelism. According to George Barna, the lifestyle of the minister or ministry leader is important. "In successful churches, people were encouraged to articulate the vision through lifestyle, not just the repetition of the right words."[81]

It is important for the minister who desires to have a fruitful ministry to have a lifestyle that includes the empowerment of the Holy Ghost to dictate vision. Even the scriptures were written by men who were carried along by the Holy

---

[81]George Barna, "It's a Vision," in *Vision for Ministry in the 21st Century*, Aubrey Malphurs (Grand Rapids: Baker House Publishing, 1994) 107.

Spirit.[82] The history of Pentecost in the last two thousand years has demonstrated the mighty potential for great ministry and witness with the equipping of the Holy Ghost baptism.

---

[82] 2 Peter 1:21.

CHAPTER 5

"The Sweet Life"

In talking about being led by the Spirit, we have endeavored to include a theological as well as a practical look at what the Bible says about following the leadership of the Holy Spirit. Although I believe, as I have frequently stated in this book, that our human nature does not lend itself automatically to leadership, our willingness to allow ourselves to be led will lead to a sweeter, more enjoyable and powerful life.

"There is a power which exists in the church akin to that which enabled Jesus to speak peace to the storm in Mark 4. It is a wind stopping, sea calming, awe inspiring power."[83] The power of God is experienced as we humble ourselves. James writes in James 4:10, *"Humble yourselves before the Lord, and he will lift you up."* Peter writes in 1 Peter 5:6, *"Humble yourselves, therefore, under God's mighty hand, that he may lift you up in due time."* Perhaps the reason why so many are unwilling to be led is because there is a fear of loss or missing out. These two passages assure us that nothing will be lost when we allow ourselves to be led by the Spirit of God.

---

[83]Wiley Hughes, *"The Visible Jesus,"* Destiny Now World Outreach Center, 2010. 18-19.

The church I pastor just completed the construction of a new worship and educational facility. The building program lasted almost 4 years. Looking back on the whole effort, I value the leadership of the Holy Spirit more than anything else

Although God gave us many gifted, resourceful, and wise people to help us and guide us, it was the Spirit Himself who led the way during the whole process. Perhaps I will never forget walking through the shell of the building, over a year from its completion with no obvious way to continue, and asking God for the provision to complete it. God spoke to me and said, "you already have what you need in your hand." What I heard God saying was that there was nothing else I needed from Him to complete the project, all I needed to do was to continue to trust Him and follow the Spirit. It was at that time that I laid aside my experience, education, and minute amount of knowledge I possessed and totally gave in to God. Now we are worshipping in the new building and it is wonderful!

I learned 3 valuable lessons from the experience of building our new "Faith Building." First, I realized the truth of what Paul writes in Hebrews 12:2 when he says, *"Let us fix our eyes on Jesus, the author and perfecter of our faith, who for the joy set before him endured the cross, scorning its shame, and sat down at the right hand of the throne of God."* Things are better when I let Jesus start them and finish them. Jesus will not start something in my life that is not going to be helpful to me and He will finish every good work He has begun in me, according to Philippians 1:6. *"… being confident of this, that he who began a good work in you will carry it on to completion until the day of Christ Jesus."*

Second, I have found that what I "want" to do often is what God wants to do. However, how I "want" to do it is seldom how God wants to do it. The experience of this has brought new realization for me to the words in Proverbs 16:25 when Solomon writes, *"There is a way that seems right to a man, but in the end it leads to death."* God's desires become our desires when we begin to "delight" ourselves in Him. However, desires and a willingness to be led by the Spirit to accomplish those desires are two very different things. He is how I have learned to compromise the two.

As I pursue a God-given desire and find myself lacking in some area to see it through to the end, I begin to look around me to see what

I possess to enable the completion of it. It's like the way God told Moses how to use the rod He carried to assist in the release of the children of Israel from Egypt.

The Third thing I have learned is that God still speaks to His people. There is still a small voice that whispers to us words of direction, guidance, and wisdom. We need to listen to that voice and to those words. The words of the enemy are counterfeit. They endeavor to lure us away from being led by the Spirit with promises he cannot keep. In Matthew 4, the third temptation of Christ was with something Jesus already possessed. In verses 8 and 9

Satan tries to tempt our Lord, *"8 Again, the devil took him to a very high mountain and showed him all the kingdoms of the world and their splendor. 9 "All this I will give you," he said, "if you will bow down and worship me."* Here, the devil is bargaining with something that doesn't belong to him. Ironically, the Scriptures tell us that the kings of the world belong to Christ. Revelation 11:15 says, *"15 The seventh angel sounded his trumpet, and there were loud voices in heaven, which said: "The kingdom of the world has become the kingdom of our Lord and of his Christ, and he will reign forever and ever."*

The point is this; you already have everything you need to be successful and live a blessed life. It's in your hand. It's in your heart. It's the leadership of the Spirit of God! Go with God and you will never go without. I encourage you to pay attention to the voice of the Spirit and though it may be difficult at times to follow, be led by the Spirit!

BIBLIOGRAPHY
In order of appearance

"Rewards of Service," in *1500 Illustrations for Biblical Preaching* ed., Michael P. Green (Grand Rapids, MI: Baker 2001) 332.

Unless otherwise indicated all Bible references in this book are to the New International Version–Updated (NIV) (Grand Rapids: Zondervan, 1984).

"Study Notes," *Key Word Study Bible*, ed., Spiros Zodhiates (Chattanooga, TN: AMG 1990) 324-235.

Thompson K. Mathew, "Ministry Defined," in *Spirit-Led Ministry in the 21st Century* (Xulon Press 2004) 18.

William Hendriksen, "Matthew," *New Testament Commentary* (Grand rapids, MI: Baker 1973) x,153, 197, 233.

Henry Blackaby, *Experiencing God*, Baptist Press (17 May 2005).

Everett F. Harrison, "Romans," *The Expositor's Bible Commentary,* vol. 10 ed. Frank E. Gaebelein. (Zondervan, Grand Rapids, 1976), 127.

D.A. Carson. Douglas J. Moo, and Leon Morris, "Romans," *An Introduction to the New Testament*, (Zondervan, Grand Rapids, 1992). 241.

Dan Britts, "Lord, Teach Us to Pray," *Davis Chinese Christian Church,* Davis, CA. http://d-ccc.org/sermons /db010503.htm. (10 November 2010).

Spiros Zodhiates, "Notes on Ephesians 4," in *Hebrew-Greek Key Word Study Bible*, NASB (Chattanooga, TN, AMG Publishers 1990). 1565.

Spiros Zodhiates, "Notes on Ephesians," in *Hebrew-Greek Key Word Study Bible*, NASB (Chattanooga, TN, AMG Publishers 1990).1560.

Skevington A.Wood, *Ephesians through Philemon*. The Expositor's Bible Commentary. Vol. 11. Frank E. Gaebelein, ed. (Grand Rapids: MI: Zondervan) 31.

F.F. Bruce, Ephesus: "Open Door and Many Adversaries," in *Paul: Apostle of the Heart Set Free*. (Grand Rapids, MI: Eerdmans Publishing, 1977) 286.

Skevington A.Wood, *Ephesians through Philemon*. The Expositor's Bible Commentary. Vol. 11. Frank E. Gaebelein, ed. (Grand Rapids: MI: Zondervan) 16.

Skevington A. Wood, 16.

Paul Trebilco, "The Early Christians in Ephesus, from Paul to Ignatius."

Lewis S. Chafer, "Ecclesiology: The Church As An Organism," in *Chafer Systematic Theology*, Vol. 4. (Dallas, TX: Dallas Seminary Press, 1948, Revised, 1975) 152.

Lewis S. Chafer, 152.

Thompson K. Mathew, *Challenges Of The New Century*, in "Spirit-Led Ministry in the 21st Century." (Xulon Press, 2004) 67.

Kevin J. Conner, *The Church in the New Testament*, (Portland OR: City Bible Publishing, 1982). 175.

Notes on Ephesians, Hebrew-Greek Key Word Study Bible-NIV. Edited by Spiros Zodhiates and warren Baker. (Chattanooga, TN: AMG International, 1996) 1368.

William Hendriksen, *Exposition of Ephesians* in "New Testament Commentary-Galatians, Ephesians, Philippians, Colossians, and Philemon." (Grand Rapids, MI: Baker Academic, 2007) 32.

Harold W. Hoehner, "Ephesians." *The Bible Knowledge Commentary-New Testament Edition.* Edited byJohn F. Walvoord and Roy B Zuck. (USA, Canada, England: Victor Books, 1983.) 614.

John Chrysostom, *Nicene and Post-Nicene Fathers*. Vol. 13. Edited by Philip Schaff. (Peabody Mass: Hendrickson, 2004) 102.

Merriam-Webster, "*Conjunction*," Webster's Ninth New collegiate Dictionary, (Springfield, Mass: Merriam-Webster Publishing, 1987), 277.

Strongs G1161, "de" in *Blue Letter Bible* 1996-2010 (6 September 2009) < http://ww.blueletterbible.org/lang /lexicon/lexicon.cfm? (9 September 2010).

Skevington Wood A., *Ephesians through Philemon*. The Expositor's Bible Commentary. Vol. 11. (Grand Rapids: MI: Zondervan, 1981), 57.

Doug Beacham, *Introduction* in "Rediscovering the Role of Apostles and Prophets." (Franklin Springs, GA: LifeSprings Resources, 2004), viii.

Strongs G305, "*anabainō*" in *Blue Letter Bible* 1996-2010 (6 September 2009) < http://www.blueletterbible.org/lang /lexicon/lexicon.cfm? (11 September 2010).

James Modlish, "Ephesians Four," The Bible Study Page, 20 October 2010 http://www.thebiblestudypage.com/eph_4.shtml. (15 November 2010).

"Gifts," blueletterbible.org Lexicon,
   http://www.blueletterbible.org/
   Bible.cfm?b=Eph&c=4&t= NASB#conc/8 (14
   November 2010).

Charis, "Lexical Aids to the New Testament," *Hebrew-Greek Key Word Study Bible*, ed., Spiros Zodhiates, (Chattanooga, TN., AMG Publishers, 1990) 1887.

"πληρόω," "Theological Dictionary of the New Testament," ed., Gerhard Friedrich, Vol. 6 (Grand Rapids, MI., Eerdmans 1968) 291.

Poimen, "Lexical Aids to the New Testament," *Hebrew-Greek Key Word Study Bible*, ed., Spiros Zodhiates, (Chattanooga, TN., AMG Publishers, 1990) 1869.

Michael D. Marlowe, "An English Guide to the Various Readings of the Greek New Testament." http://www.bible-researcher.com/ephesians.html (15 November 2010).

A. Skevington Wood, "Ephesians through Philemon," in *The Expositor's Bible Commentary*, vol.11. ed., Frank E.Gaebelein, (Grand Rapids: Zondervan, 1981)20.

D.A. Carson, Douglas J. Moo, Leon Morris, "Ephesians," in *An Introduction to the New Testament* (Grand Rapids, Zondervan 1992). 312.

A. Skevington Wood, 57.

James Burton Coffman, "Commentary on Ephesians 4,"http:// www.searchgodsword.org/com/bcc/view.cgi?book= ephchapter=004>.Abilene, Texas, USA. 1983- 1999. (15 November 2010).

"δίδωμι didōmi"http://www.blueletterbible.org/lang/lexicon /lexicon.cfm?Strongs=G1325&t=NASB (15 November 2010).

John A. Mackay, "The Fullness of Christ" in *God's Order- The Ephesians Letter and This Present Time* (New York, NY: McMillan Company, 1953) 149.

Robert H. Gundry, "The Prison Epistles of Paul," in *A Survey of the New Testament* (Grand Rapids, MI: Zondervan, 1981) 294.

Friedrick D. E. Schleiermacher, "Einleitung in das Neue Testament," in *Sammtliche Werke*, ed. G. Wolde (Berlin: G. Reimer, 1845), 1:165, 166.

A Skevington Wood, "Ephesians," in *The Expositor's Bible Commentary*, ed., Vol., 11 Frank E. Gaebelein (Grand Rapids, MI: Zondervan, 1981) 15.

F.F. Bruce, "Ephesus: Open Door and Many Adversaries," in *Paul Apostle of the Heart Set Free*, (Grand Rapids: Eerdmans 1977) 291.

Flavius Josephus, "The Antiquities of the Jews," in *The Works of Josephus*, Book 14, Chapter 10, translated, William Whiston (Peabody, MA: Hendrickson) 382.

George Barlow, "The Epistle To The Ephesians," in *The Preacher's Homiletic Commentary*, vol. 28 (Grand Rapids, MI: Baker, 1996) 123.

D.A. Carson, Douglas J. Moo, Leon Morris, "Ephesians," in *An Introduction to the New Testament* (Grand Rapids, MI: Zondervan, 1992.) 306.

Sidney Greidanus, "Preaching Epistles," in *The Modern Preacher and the Ancient Text-Interpreting and Preaching Biblical Literature* (Grand Rapids, MI: Eerdmans, 1988) 314-315.

Sidney Greidanus, 315.

Neil Ormerod, "On the Divine Institution of the Three-fold Ministry" in *"Ecclesiology"* (Strathfield, AUS Brill Academic Publishers2007).

Augustine, "On Christian Doctrine," in *City of God* Nicene and Post-Nicene Fathers-1st Edition (Grand rapids, MI: Hendrickson, 2004) 585.

John Calvin, "Epistle to the Ephesians," in *John Calvin's Commentaries* (Grand Rapids, MI: Baker 2003) 280.

"ποιμή v" Theological Dictionary of the New Testament," ed., Kittel, Vol. 5 (Grand Rapids, MI., Eerdmans 1968) 497.

Lewis Sperry Chaffer, "Ecclesiology: "The Church as an Organism," in *Chaffer Systematic Theology* (Dallas, TX: Dallas Seminary Press, 1980) 152.

John A. Mackay, "The Fullness of Christ," in *The Ephesian Letter and this Present Time* (New York, NY: The Macmillan Company, 1953) 149.

Terry Tramel, "The Empowerment of the Holy Spirit," in *The Beauty of The Balance* (Franklin Springs, GA: Lifesprings Resources, 2009), 180.

Thom Rainer, "Toward the Twenty-First Century, 1988 to the Future," in *The Book of Church Growth* (Nashville, TN; Broadman and Holman Publishers 1993), 62.

Allison Kidd Covington, "Why Pentecostal? A Look at the Phenomenon of Rapid Pentecostal Growth in Latin America," http://inquiry.uark.edu/Covington_Final_for_Online.pdf (12 December 2009) 11.

Dick Eastmen, "Developing a Prayer Ministry in the Local Church," *The Pentecostal Pastor* Unit 3, Preparing for Revival, ed. Thomas E. Trask, Wayde I. Goodall, and Zenas J. Bicket (Springfield, MI; Gospel Publishing Co., 2000) 237.

Thom Rainer, "Signs and Wonders and Church Growth," in *The Book of Church Growth* (Nashville, TN; Broadman and Holman Publishers 1993), 303.

C. Peter Wagner, "The 'Why' of the New Wineskins," *Churchquake*, (Ventura, CA. Regal Publishing, 1999) 11.

Jessica Ravitz, Moved by The Spirit: Fastest Growing Pentecostal Church Takes Root in the 'Last Frontier'. *Religion News Blog* (5 May 2006) The Salt Lake Tribune USA

Thom Rainer, "Why Good is Not Enough: The Chrysalis Factor," in *Breakout Churches* (Grand Rapids: MI, Zondervan Publishing, 2005) 27.

Gary B. McGee, To the Regions Beyond: "The Global Expansion of Pentecost," in *The Century of the Holy Spirit by Vinson Synan,* (Nashville, TN: Thomas Nelson Publishing, 2001) 69.

Gordon L. Anderson, "Signs and Wonders," in *The Pentecostal Pastor* Unit 3, Preparing for Revival, ed. Thomas E. Trask, Wayde I. Goodall, and Zenas J. Bicket (Springfield, MI; Gospel Publishing Co., 2000) 303.

C. Samuel Storms, "A Third Wave View," in *Are Miraculous Gifts for Today?* ed., Wayne Grudem and Stanley Gundry. (Grand Rapids: Zondervan 1996) 188.

Gordon L. Anderson, Pentecostal Hermeneutics Part Two, AG Churches.org, http://agchurches.org/Sitefiles/Default/RSS/IValue/Resources/Holy%20Spirit/Articles/PentecostalHermeneuticsPt2.pdf. (14 December 2009) 5.

Gary L. McIntosh and R. Daniel Reeves, "Life-Giving System 1: Pastor's Spiritual Life," in *Thriving Churches in the Twenty-first Century* (Grand Rapids: Kregel Publications, 2006) 48.

Gary B. McGee, "Baptism of the Holy Ghost and Fire! The Revival Legacy of Minnie F. Abrams" *Enrichment Journal* http://enrichmentjournal. ag.org/199803/080_baptism_fire.cfm.(14 December 2009).

Malcolm McDow, "The Southwestern Story," in *Revival* ed. John Avant, Malcolm, Alvin Reid (Nashville,TN: Broadman and Holman Publishers, 1996) 70.

Wikipedia, Joel Osteen, (28 November 2009) http://en.wikipedia.org/wiki/Joel_Osteen (14 December 2009).

John B. Polhill, *Acts*, New American Commentary (Nashville; Boardman, 1992), 106.

Vinson Synan, The Pentecostal Century: An Overview in *The Century of the Holy Spirit by Vinson Synan,* (Nashville, TN: Thomas Nelson Publishing, 2001) 5.

Cary McMullen, "Pentecostals Celebrate World's Fastest Growing Religion," The Ledger.com, http://www.theledger.com/article/20060424/NEWS/604240374?Title=Pentecostals-Celebrate-World-s-Fastest-Growing-Religion (14 December 2009).

C. Peter Wagner, "Protestantism's New Look," *Churchquake*, (Ventura, CA. Regal Publishing, 1999) 47-48.

George Barna, "It's a Vision," in *Vision for Ministry in the 21st Century*, Aubrey Malphurs (Grand Rapids: Baker House Publishing, 1994) 107.

Wiley Hughes, *"The Visible Jesus,"* Destiny Now World Outreach Center, 2010. 18-19.

Notes

[171]

[172]

[174]

[175]

www.ingramcontent.com/pod-product-compliance
Lightning Source LLC
Chambersburg PA
CBHW060753050426
42449CB00008B/1390